BODY WORKS™

BREATH
The Respiratory System

Gillian Houghton

PowerKiDS
press

New York

Published in 2007 by The Rosen Publishing Group, Inc.
29 East 21st Street, New York, NY 10010

First Edition

Editor: Amelie von Zumbusch
Book Design: Greg Tucker

Photo Credits: Cover, pp. 14, 17 (left) © 3D Clinic/Getty Images; p. 5 © Bo Veisland, Mi & I/Photo Researchers, Inc.; p. 6 © Stephen Frink/Corbis; p. 9 © J. Bavosi/Photo Researchers, Inc.; p. 10 (left) © Zephyr/Photo Researchers, Inc.; p. 10 (right) © Hans-Ulrich Osterwalder/Photo Researchers, Inc.; p. 13 (left) © John M. Dougherty/Photo Researchers, Inc.; p. 13 (right) © David M. Martin/Photo Researchers, Inc.; p. 17 (right) © Martin M. Rotker/Photo Researchers, Inc.; p. 18 (left) © Kai Pfaffenbach/Reuters/Corbis; p. 18 (right) © Veronique Estiot/Photo Researchers, Inc.; p. 21 (top) © Michael Keller/Corbis; p. 18 (left) © Patrik Giardino/Corbis.

Library of Congress Cataloging-in-Publication Data

Houghton, Gillian.
  Breath : the respiratory system / Gillian Houghton.— 1st ed.
      p. cm. — (Body works)
  Includes index.
  ISBN (10) 1-4042-3471-3 (13) 978-1-4042-3471-0 (library binding) — ISBN (10) 1-4042-2180-8 (13) 978-1-4042-2180-2 (pbk.)
  1. Respiratory organs—Juvenile literature. 2. Respiration—Juvenile literature. I. Title. II. Series.
  QP121.H74 2007
  612.2—dc22
                                    2005035701

Manufactured in the United States of America

Contents

The Respiratory System

    The respiratory system is made up of the parts of the body that help in breathing. We breathe in air. This air travels through a long, tunnel-like **airway** to the **lungs**. The lungs take in **oxygen** from the air. They also let go of an unsafe gas called **carbon dioxide**. The carbon dioxide moves up the airways and leaves the body when we breathe out. This trade of oxygen and carbon dioxide happens thousands of times each day. Most of the time we do not notice it. However, we could not live without it.

Nose

Mouth

Larynx

Medulla Oblongata

Trachea

Lungs

The different parts of the respiratory system work together to keep the body breathing and healthy.

People need to breathe in oxygen several times a minute. When people swim deep underwater, they have to carry a tank of oxygen to breathe.

Oxygen and Carbon Dioxide

Every cell in the body needs oxygen to do its work. We get oxygen from the air. When we breathe in, air fills our lungs. Our lungs have thousands of **blood vessels**. Blood in the lungs takes in oxygen from the air. The blood carries oxygen throughout the body using the **circulatory system**.

The body's cells produce carbon dioxide as they work. Too much carbon dioxide is unsafe for the body. Blood carries carbon dioxide to the lungs and lets it go. The carbon dioxide moves through the airways. It leaves the body when a person breathes out.

The Nose and the Mouth

The nose is made of two cavities, or open spaces. They are covered by bone and **cartilage**. The nose's cavities are lined with a thin coating of mucus. Mucus is a slimy **liquid**. It helps trap dust and other tiny bits of matter that enter our noses with the air. This action cleans the air. It makes air healthier and easier for us to breathe.

People breathe through both their noses and their mouths. You can breathe through your mouth when your nose is stuffed up.

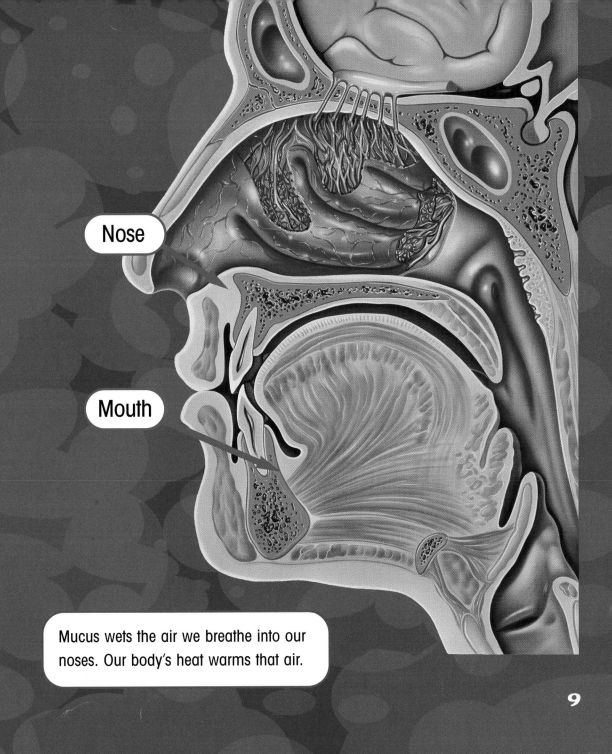

Nose

Mouth

Mucus wets the air we breathe into our noses. Our body's heat warms that air.

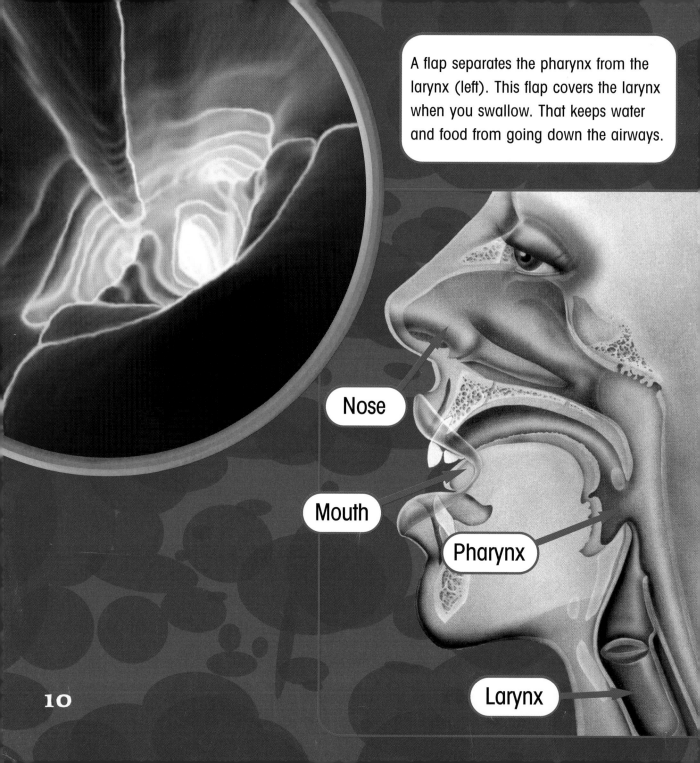

A flap separates the pharynx from the larynx (left). This flap covers the larynx when you swallow. That keeps water and food from going down the airways.

Nose

Mouth

Pharynx

Larynx

The Pharynx and the Larynx

The **pharynx** is a tunnel of **muscle** that ties the nose and mouth to the **larynx**. The larynx is made of muscle and cartilage. Inside the larynx there are two folds called the vocal cords.

When we prepare to speak, the muscles of the larynx contract, or press together. The vocal cords are pulled together tightly. Then we breathe out and the air pushes against our vocal cords. This makes the vocal cords vibrate, or shake. This vibration produces sound. Movements in the mouth turn this sound into words.

The Trachea and the Bronchi ——

The **trachea** lies below the larynx. The trachea divides, or branches off, into two smaller tunnels of cartilage called **bronchi**. Each bronchi leads to one of the body's two lungs. There the bronchi divide. These smaller bronchi reach every part of the lung. The bronchi continue to divide into smaller parts, like the branches of a tree. The smallest bronchi are called bronchioles.

Large blood vessels enter the lungs alongside the bronchi. These blood vessels divide into smaller and smaller tunnels called capillaries.

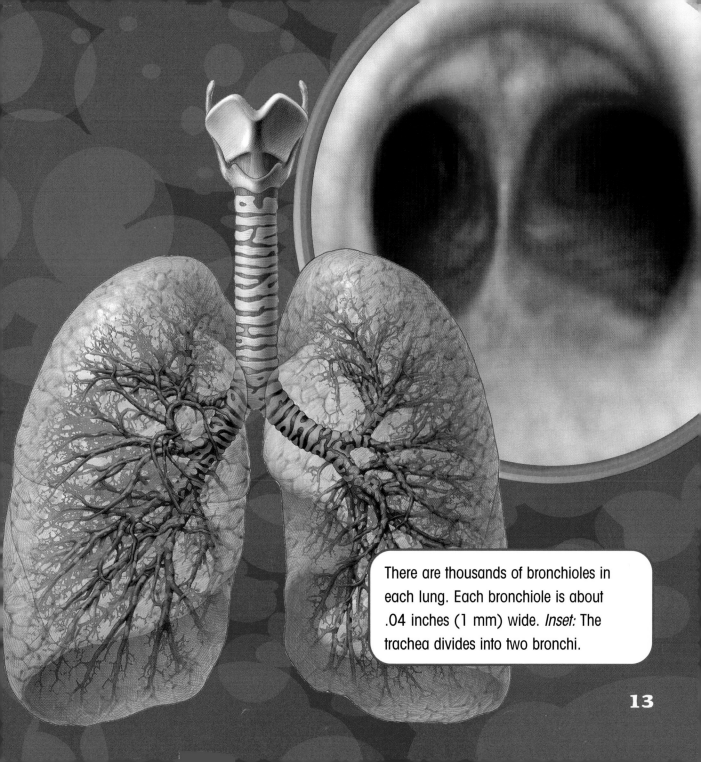

There are thousands of bronchioles in each lung. Each bronchiole is about .04 inches (1 mm) wide. *Inset:* The trachea divides into two bronchi.

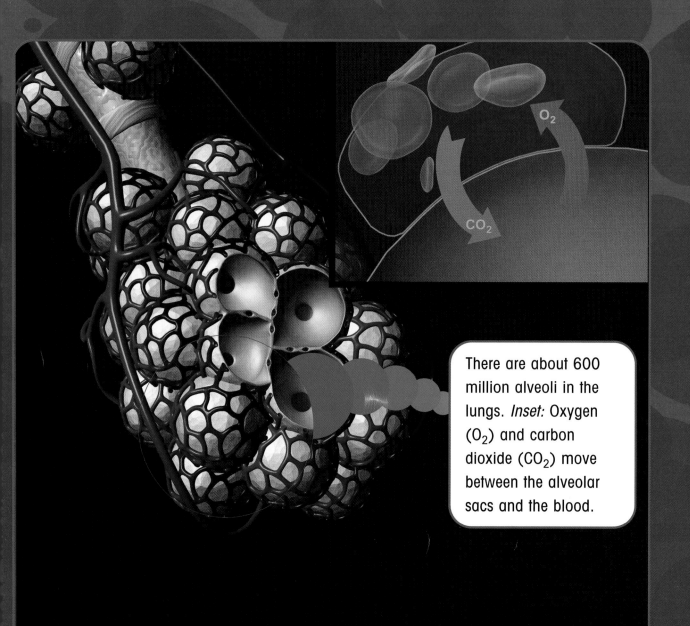

There are about 600 million alveoli in the lungs. *Inset:* Oxygen (O_2) and carbon dioxide (CO_2) move between the alveolar sacs and the blood.

Inside the Lungs

Inside the lungs each bronchiole ends in a group of tiny, round pouches, called alveolar sacs. A web of capillaries covers each pouch. The walls of the alveolar sacs are thin. They let oxygen pass through them to the capillaries. In the capillaries blood takes in oxygen. The blood leaves the lungs and carries oxygen to the body's cells.

Carbon dioxide from the blood moves through the walls of the alveolar sacs into the lungs. The carbon dioxide leaves the lungs through the bronchi. It travels through airways and then out of the nose or the mouth.

Take a Deep Breath

The lungs are inside a group of bones called the rib cage. The rib cage and its muscles form the walls of the chest cavity. A strong muscle called the diaphragm forms the cavity's bottom. When we prepare to take a breath, a part of the brain called the medulla oblongata sends a message to the chest muscles. It tells the muscles to contract. When the muscles contract, they push the ribs out and up. The chest cavity widens. This allows the lungs to fill with air. Filling the lungs with air is called inhalation.

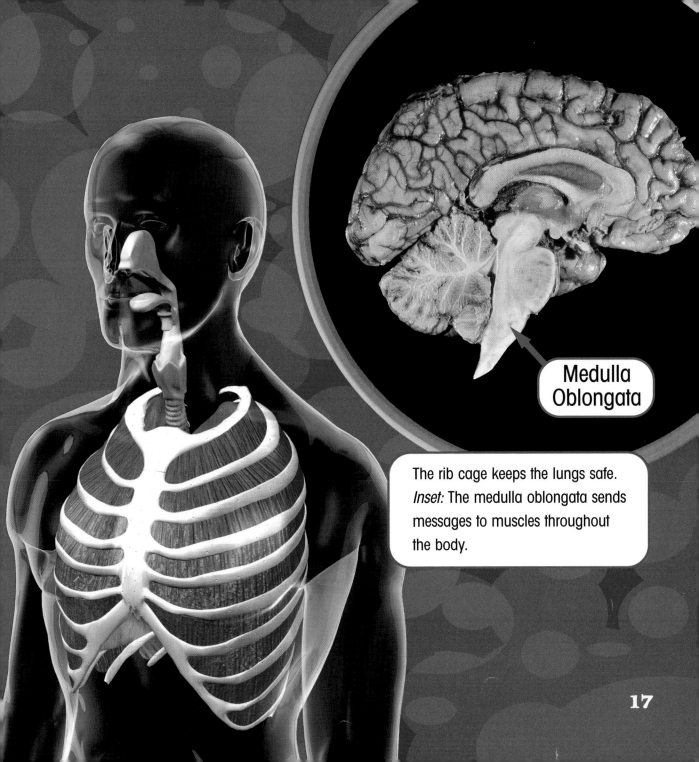

Medulla
Oblongata

The rib cage keeps the lungs safe.
Inset: The medulla oblongata sends
messages to muscles throughout
the body.

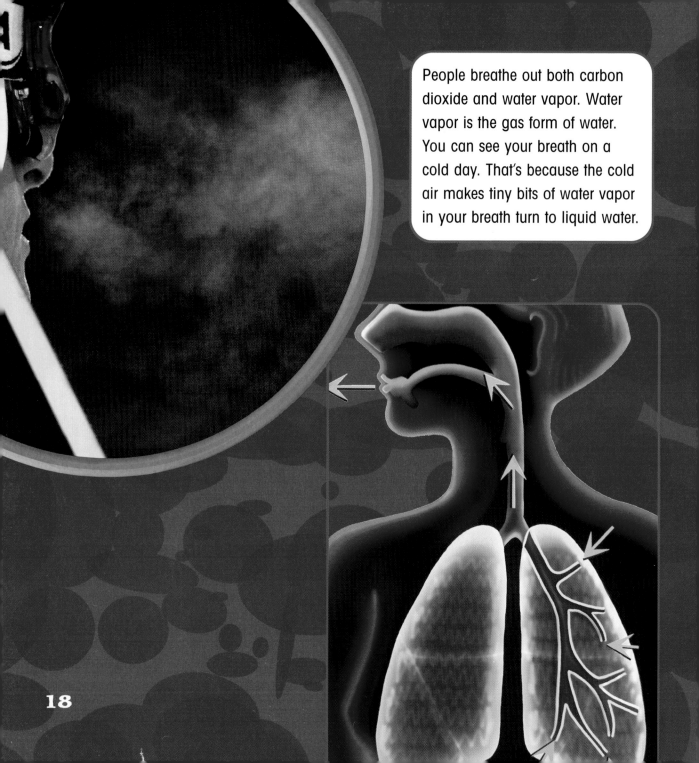

People breathe out both carbon dioxide and water vapor. Water vapor is the gas form of water. You can see your breath on a cold day. That's because the cold air makes tiny bits of water vapor in your breath turn to liquid water.

Then Let It Out

During exhalation we breathe out air. Our chest muscles relax, or rest. This draws the rib cage in and down. The chest cavity becomes smaller. This action forces the lungs to let out the air inside them. The air is pushed through the airways and out of the nose or the mouth.

Most of the air is pushed out of the lungs when we breathe out. There is always a little air left in the lungs, though. The little air that stays in the lungs helps them keep their shape.

Just Breathe

Breathing is most often an involuntary action. This means we breathe without planning to take each breath. As you sit reading this book, you are taking between 12 and 18 breaths each minute. When you exercise, your muscles need more oxygen. This is why you breathe more often or more deeply when you exercise.

Coughing and sneezing are also involuntary respiratory actions. Coughing and sneezing get rid of dust and other matter in the respiratory system. Coughing cleans out the airways. A sneeze cleans out the nose's cavities.

Exercise, like playing soccer, makes the body need extra oxygen. For that reason a person exercising takes more breaths each minute than a person sitting does. *Inset:* Sneezing cleans out the nose. This makes it easier to breathe.

Respiratory Trouble

Bacteria are one-celled living things. They can live in the respiratory system. Bacteria cause respiratory sicknesses, such as bronchitis. **Viruses** can take over cells in the respiratory system and make a person sick. For example, you can catch a cold or flu virus. Respiratory illnesses are also caused by low **tidal volume**. One such illness is asthma. Asthma makes the airways narrow. It keeps enough air from reaching the lungs.

Smoking also causes respiratory problems. When people smoke, they breathe unsafe matter into their lungs. This destroys the walls of the alveolar sacs.

Glossary

airway (AYR-way) The tunnel for air that ties the nose or mouth to the lungs.

blood vessels (BLUD VEH-suhlz) Tunnels in the body through which blood flows.

bronchi (BRON-kee) Two tunnels in the chest that bring air to each of the lungs.

carbon dioxide (KAR-bin dy-OK-syd) A gas that the body makes to get rid of waste.

cartilage (KAR-tuh-lij) The bendable matter from which a person's nose and ears are made.

circulatory system (SER-kyuh-luh-tor-ee SIS-tehm) The path by which blood travels through the body.

larynx (LER-inks) The space between the pharynx and the trachea.

liquid (LIH-kwed) Matter that moves like water.

lungs (LUNGZ) The parts of an air-breathing animal that take in air and supply oxygen to the blood.

muscle (MUH-sul) A part of the body that is used to make the body move.

oxygen (OK-sih-jen) A gas that has no color or taste and is necessary for people and animals to breathe.

pharynx (FA-rinks) A tunnel of muscle that ties the mouth to the larynx.

tidal volume (TY-dul VOL-yoom) How much air a person breathes in and out.

trachea (TRAY-kee-uh) The pipe that brings air down toward the lungs.

viruses (VY-rus-ez) Tiny things that cause an illness.

Index

A
alveolar sacs, 15, 22
asthma, 22

B
blood, 7, 15
blood vessels, 7, 12
bronchi, 12, 15

C
carbon dioxide, 4, 7, 15
cell(s), 7, 15

D
diaphragm, 16

L
larynx, 11–12
lungs, 4, 7, 12, 15–16, 19, 22

M
mouth, 8, 11, 15
mucus, 8

N
nose, 8, 15

O
oxygen, 4, 7, 15, 20

P
pharynx, 11

R
rib cage, 16, 19

T
trachea, 12

V
vocal cords, 11

Web Sites

Due to the changing nature of Internet links, PowerKids Press has developed an online list of Web sites related to the subject of this book. This site is updated regularly. Please use this link to access the list:

www.powerkidslinks.com/hybw/respirat/